Made in the USA
Las Vegas, NV
19 July 2024

92627223R00057